Toilet Training Your Child with Special Needs

A Guide for Parents

Juliet Hawkins, MA, LMHC

PAGE PUBLISHING
Conneaut Lake, PA

First originally published by Page Publishing 2023

ISBN 979-8-88654-252-3 (pbk)
ISBN 979-8-88654-253-0 (digital)

Printed in the United States of America

Contents

Introduction

I have been working in the field of developmental disabilities for over thirty years. When I interview parents to determine their needs, toilet training is one of the major ones that they identify.

I believe that almost every child, regardless of his diagnosis or level of functioning, is capable of being taught to use the bathroom. However, every child is unique and, therefore, has his own rate of progress. Progress is rarely a straight line. It is normal for there to be ups and downs.

Teaching your child to use the bathroom independently is a major developmental milestone. You are not merely teaching your child a skill. You are teaching your child responsibility. You are teaching your child how to make choices. You are changing your child's role in the family from one of dependence to one of interdependence. There are unique challenges that you may be facing. Maybe your child doesn't seem to mind that he is wet or soiled. Maybe your child doesn't want to sit on the toilet. Not surprisingly, you may be finding that the old-fashioned, tried-and-true methods that seem to work with typically developing children don't seem to work with your child.

There's a saying that if it ain't broke, then don't fix it. So if you are having success with toilet training your child, then by all means, continue what you are doing. This book is meant for those of you who are facing challenges. You might just be thinking of toilet training your child, but don't have a clue of where to begin. You might have already begun, but are having no success. You may have toilet trained your child, but now find that she is suddenly regressing. No matter where you are in the process, I hope that this book can be of value to you.

No matter where you and your child are in this process, stick with the plan. Don't be discouraged if there are obstacles. In fact, I will go as far as to say that you should expect there to be obstacles and be pleasantly surprised if there is smooth sailing. Don't give up. Patience and perseverance are the keys to success!

Getting Ready

One of the hardest things for a parent to determine is whether or not their child is "ready" for toilet training. They look for signs from their child to indicate that he is ready. In typically developing children, some signs may be the following: (a) they start taking off their diaper, (b) they act disturbed if they are wet or soiled, (c) they begin imitating other family members, or (d) they actually start asking to go to the bathroom.

Often, children with special needs don't show these signs. Some children don't seem to care whether or not they are wet or soiled. Some have significant receptive and expressive language deficits. Some children barely make eye contact.

So does that mean that your child is not ready? Not necessarily. In my experience, there are two main factors that determine if your child is ready for toilet training:

a. He has developed the muscular control needed to retain his urine or bowel movements.
b. There are no medical issues that would be a deterrent.

Everything else can be taught. Your child can be taught to distinguish between wet and dry. Your child can be taught to communicate that he has to go the bathroom.

Just as important as figuring out whether or not your child is ready is deciding whether or not *you* are ready. Toilet training is a joint venture. There is a part that you play and part that your child plays. You want to make sure that you set yourself and your child up for success. Some suggestions for getting ready are as follows:

A. Discuss your plan to toilet train your child with other significant adults. This may mean your spouse, an extended family member, a teacher, a therapist, or a physician.

B. You want to gather all your materials. In general, I suggest that you get an egg timer, a large supply of underwear, and pull ups (to be used when your child does not have access to the bathroom).

C. Make sure that you have the proper mindset.

- Be prepared for things to be harder in the beginning. Even though you want your child to be toilet trained, it often seems easier to change a diaper than to deal with accidents. Teaching your child to do something for herself means that you have to be prepared for your child to make mistakes.

- Be prepared to make mistakes yourself. You and your child are both learning new skills. Mistakes are part of learning.

- Avoid comparing your child with other children. Your child is an individual.

-   Develop a stress management plan for yourself.

Your follow-up

1. Discuss toilet training with significant adults involved in your child's life. If you are just beginning, then discuss your desire to toilet train your child. If you have already begun and are experiencing problems, then discuss these problems with significant adults.
2. Begin stocking up on needed materials.
3. Get your child medically evaluated to determine that there are no medical obstacles.

Keeping Track
of Things

One of the most important things that you can do is to keep a written record of your child's progress. This is something that you should plan to do as soon as you make the commitment to begin toilet training. Keeping a written record is the best way to measure your child's progress, objectively.

Tracking your child's toileting patterns before beginning toilet training will help you plan more effectively. For example, you may notice that your child has bowel movements at certain times. You might notice that your child behaves in a certain manner before she urinates or has a bowel movement. Keeping a written record of your child's progress will help you to be more observant.

Keeping a written record is nothing new. For example, writing down your expenditures helps you budget your money more effectively. Keeping a record of weight helps you know if your diet is working. Journaling is becoming increasingly popular.

Once you begin toilet training, you should continue to keep a written track of your child's progress. This helps in many ways. It helps to identify possible areas of challenge. It also helps you know *objectively* what direction things are moving in. Often, it is difficult to detect your child's progress one way or the other. If you depend on your subjective feeling about how things are going, you may miss the fact that your child is actually making progress. The difference between having four accidents a day and three accidents is often not detectable unless you are keeping a written record of your child's progress.

Some important things that you want to track is when your child urinates and when your child has a bowel movement. You also want to track when your child urinates or has a bowel movement in the toilet.

Keeping a written record doesn't have to be complicated or tedious. In the appendix, I have provided you with two sample data sheets that I have used in my interventions. The data sheet in Appendix A has three columns. The first column lists times in five-minute intervals from 7:00 a.m. to 9:55 p.m. The second column is used to record anything that your child does in the toilet. The third column is used to record anything that happens outside the toilet (accidents). You should use a separate data sheet for each day. For example, if your child has a urine accident at 3:45 p.m., you find "3:45 p.m." in the first column. You should write a *U* in the third column. The advantage of using this type of data sheet is that it can be used during any phase of the intervention. It can be used before you begin training, when you are trying to see if there is any pattern. It can be used during training to track any progress. The goal is to see an increase in what is written in the second column and a decrease in what is recorded in the third column.

The data sheet in Appendix B is best used when you are attempting to get your child to use the toilet (whether or not you have begun formal training).

As you can see, both data sheets do not involve a lot of writing and are both simple. Either you can use one of these data sheets or you can develop one of your own. The important thing is to develop a system for keeping track.

Your follow-up

Decide upon a tracking system that you will use. Start using it right away, no matter what phase you are in.

Breaking Things Down

We have been talking about toilet training as if it was just one task. However, in reality, toilet training is made up of a series of tasks. Identifying these tasks is called a *task analysis*. Breaking things down not only makes it easier to teach, but it will help you identify where you are getting stuck. First, I will list the tasks of toilet training. Then I will explain some of these tasks:

1. Communicate that it is time to go to the bathroom.
2. Travel to the bathroom.
3. Pull down pants.
4. Sit on toilet (for five minutes or when your child has voided—whichever happens first).
5. Stand up.

6. Wipe, if necessary.
7. Pull up pants.
8. Flush toilet (only if your child has voided).
9. Wash hands.
10. Prompt your child to engage in a positive, structured activity.

Communication

This is an especially important step in the process. You want your child to let you know that she has to go to the bathroom. This is often a challenge for a child with special needs, especially if he is not verbal. By making it a part of the toilet training routine, you are teaching your child to communicate his needs. If your child is verbal, then he can be asked to say the words. If your child is nonverbal or has trouble verbalizing, then other means of communication can be used. This can include sign language, a communication device, or pictures. The most common method that I have used with parents is a picture of the toilet. Laminated pictures of the toilet can be posted in several places in your home with Velcro so that they are easily accessible to your child.

Travel to the bathroom

I decided to say "travel" to the bathroom instead of "walk" to the bathroom because some children with special needs are not ambulatory. However, this is not a deterrent to toilet training. One important thing is to make sure that your bathroom is accessible to your child.

Pull down pants and underwear

If your child is wearing pants, make sure that they are loose fitting and relatively easy to pull down or up. I do not recommend that your child walk around in only underwear if your child is three years old or older, as it is not age appropriate.

Sit on toilet for five minutes or until your child voids—whichever happens first

In case you were wondering, I am using the word "void" to refer to urinating or a bowel movement. One of the typical old-fashioned methods of toilet training is to sit your child on the toilet until "they do something," no matter how long it takes. In addition, if your child gets restless, give him a book or a toy to keep him sitting. I *do not* recommend doing any of these things for one main reason—these things won't help your child understand why she is in the bathroom, sitting on the toilet. Your child is not there to have fun or to play. Your child is there to void in the toilet. Sitting for long periods of time is counterproductive and can be aversive for your child with special needs. It can be a challenge to get some children to sit on the toilet for five minutes, much less for a longer period of time. I recommend that you buy an egg timer. Once your child is sitting on the toilet, set the timer for five minutes. If your child urinates or has a bowel movement prior to this, then you can praise her and move on to the next step. If your child has not voided within five minutes, then move on to the next step. You may be concerned about accidents. Don't worry. We'll talk about that later.

One more important point to discuss has to do with boys. There is the question of whether it is better to teach boys to stand to urinate or to start out with sitting for both urination and bowel movements. My answer to this is that it depends. If you think that it would not be too confusing to your boy, then by all means have him stand and then sit. If your child is significantly limited with regards to his ability to understand, then it may be simpler to start with sitting.

Stand up

I don't think this needs any more explanation.

Wipe, if necessary

This step is done only if your child has voided. Otherwise, there is no reason to do this. This is an important step to teach your child to do. Your child may need your physical assistance with this step. That is okay, as long as your child participates.

Flush toilet (only if your child has voided in the toilet)

I have found that many children enjoy this step. So if they void in the toilet, then by all means, they should flush the toilet. But only if they have voided. Otherwise, there is no purpose. Every step of the toileting process has a practical purpose.

Wash hands

Good hygiene is essential for your child's health. This is another step that your child may find enjoyable. However, make sure that he is actually washing his hands and not playing in the water.

Prompt your child to engage in a positive/structured activity

I recommend this for a couple of reasons. First of all, I think that all children should spend time engaged in positive/structured activities. This is especially important for children with special needs.

The other reason is that while you are in the process of toilet training your child, she will be receiving a lot of your time and attention. Children thrive on attention. However, as your child becomes more independent, she will naturally be requiring less of your attention. Some children react (unconsciously) by behaving more dependently in order to continue to receive the same level of attention. By building in time for positive structured activities other than toileting, this will ensure that your child continues to receive this positive attention from you. The activity can be something simple and does not have to be time consuming. However, it should be something that your child enjoys.

This is a good time to talk about prompts. A prompt is the level of support that your child requires in order to successfully complete a task. If your child is able to complete a task with no help from you, then we say that he is *independent* with this task. If you have to ask your child to complete a task or tell him how to do it, then we say that he needed *verbal prompting*. If you have to point in order for your child to complete a task, we say that he needed *gestural prompting*. If you have to demonstrate how to do a task in order for your child to be successful, we say that he needed *modeling.* If you have to guide your child physically in order for him to successfully complete a task, we say that he needed *physical prompting.* Some children need extensive physical help to complete a task to the point where they require *hand-over-hand prompting.*

The challenge for any parent is to provide enough support to your child, so that she is able to successfully complete a task. On the other hand, you want to avoid giving your child more help than she needs. That will interfere with the goal of independence. As you look at the tasks of toileting, you will mostly likely see that your child needs more help with some tasks and less help with others. The key is to assess your child's strengths and weaknesses.

Your follow-up

1. Using the task analysis provided in this section, assess how much prompting your child needs to complete each task. This is something that you should do whether you are just beginning toilet training, or if you are already in the process. It is helpful to take stock of where your child is at.

2. If you are already in the process of toilet training your child, then assess whether you are giving your child too much prompting, too little prompting, or the right amount of prompting to complete each task. Then increase or decrease your support accordingly.

To Reward or Not to Reward

You may be wondering if you should reward your child for going to the bathroom. The answer is, of course you should. One of the principles of behavior management is that if you want a behavior to increase, then you should reinforce it. Since you want your child to void in the toilet, it makes sense that you should reinforce your child for doing so by rewarding her.

The real question is, what kind of reward should you give your child? The most powerful reward that you can give your child is something that costs nothing and is portable. I am talking about your attention. Your attention is an enormously powerful tool you can use to increase positive behavior. So you should praise your child when he voids in the toilet. Actually, you should praise your child for each step of toileting that he completes, no matter how much help he needed to complete the task or how long it took to complete it. You should praise your child for walking to the bathroom, for pulling down his pants, and for sitting on the toilet. You should praise your child for wiping himself, flushing the toilet, and washing his hands. You should praise your child for having dry pants (more about that later). However, you should praise your child most enthusiastically every time he voids in the toilet. By giving your child this positive attention, you are letting your child know that you are approving of his behavior and want to see more of it.

To make sure that your praising is effective, you should look at your child and smile at him. You should sound enthusiastic. Most of all, you should state the behavior that you approve of. It is a lot more powerful to say "Great job, Johnny, for sitting on the toilet" than "Good boy, Johnny." This way, your child knows exactly what behavior you are approving of. It doesn't matter whether or not your child is verbal. Your child will get the message.

You may also be wondering if you should reward your child with something other than praising for voiding in the toilet. The upside of using other rewards is that it may give your child an even stronger message about what you want him to do. The downside is that you will have to eventually fade out that reward, which can be challenging. That is why I suggest that you start off by using praising as a reward. Introducing other rewards should be done only after you have tried praising for a substantial period of time without success. If you do decide to introduce another reward, make sure that it is (a) something that your child really likes, so as to be motivating, (b) something that you are able and willing to give your child, and (c) something that is not available to your child at any other time or for any other reason.

Your follow-up

1. Practice praising your child for things that you approve of. It doesn't have to be something major. It can be for something that he is already doing. Catching your child being good will get him used to receiving your attention for engaging in positive behavior. It will improve your relationship

with your child and do wonders for your child's self-esteem.

2. Start rewarding yourself. Parenting is a hard job. Parenting a child with special needs is even harder. Rewarding yourself can be something as small as taking some time to get together with a friend or watching a movie or getting your nails done. The point is, give yourself a hand for your positive efforts. It will improve your relationship with your child and do wonders for your self-esteem.

There Will Be Accidents

Let's get this out of the way. There will be accidents. In most cases, there will be many accidents, especially in the beginning. This is something that you have to be prepared to deal with. There is no learning without mistakes. Think back on when you were learning a new skill. It could be when you were a child or as an adult. Did you make mistakes? Of course. Mistakes are part of the learning process. So you have to be prepared to deal with accidents.

A crucial part of toilet training is how you respond to accidents. Toilet training is teaching your child to be responsible. You will be teaching your child to take responsibility for the choices that she makes. So if your child chooses to void in the toilet, then she should get a positive response from you. Your child will need to get a different response from you if she has an accident.

Before we go any further, some of you may be surprised when I say that your child needs to learn to take responsibility for the choices that she makes. That's right. I said that *she is making a choice*. Remember, I said that your child is ready for toilet training if she has no medical issues and has developed the muscle control to hold her urine or bowel movement. If you are not sure about this, then you need to back up and make sure. Otherwise, your child is capable of making choices. The goal is to teach your child to make positive choices. In this case, you want to teach your child to choose to void in the toilet and not outside the toilet. Don't make the mistake of underestimating your child's ability to learn just because she has special needs. The majority of children have the ability to learn how to void in the toilet.

Teaching your child to make better choices does not mean that you punish him for having an accident. In fact, if you act excited, raise your voice, or react in an angry or upset fashion, it could end up causing toileting to be an aversive activity for your child. The goal is to handle accidents in a way that encourages your child to take responsibility for the choices that he makes without damaging his self-esteem. When your child has an accident:

1. Remain calm.
2. Deal with the accident as soon as you discover it. Do so, even if it interrupts an activity.
3. In a calm but firm voice, make a statement such as "John, you made _______ [whatever

name you have chosen to call his accident]. You should do that in the toilet. Let's go to the bathroom now."

4. Then prompt your child to follow all the steps of toileting immediately.

5. Your child should participate, as much as he is capable of, in cleaning up the accident, even if he requires hand-over-hand assistance to do so successfully. Of course, if your child can do something with less assistance, he should do so, as the goal is to promote independence. Examples of tasks that your child can participate in are washing out his underwear, washing himself up, cleaning the floor, etc. Choose at least one task that your child will participate in.

6. If it is a messy bowel accident, then prompt your child to the bathroom, have your child help with cleaning himself up, and then follow the steps of toileting.

7. Remind your child that he should tell you if he has to go to the bathroom. If you are using pictures, show him the picture of the bathroom to reinforce this communication.

You might be wondering why I am suggesting that you prompt your child through all the steps of toileting even after the accident has been cleaned up. This is called positive practice. It is reminding your child what he needs to be doing.

Of course, it is easier to deal with a bowel accident in Pampers than a bowel accident in underwear or on the floor. Of course, it is easier for you to clean up an accident than to teach your child to participate. However, keep in mind that your goal is to toilet train your child, to promote independence and to teach your child responsibility. In the short term, things will seem harder. In the long term, it will be easier once your child is toilet trained. Keep your long-term goal in mind.

Your follow-up

Think of other ways that you can encourage your child to be more responsible. Pick one small task and start asking your child to do it, even if he needs prompting. Some examples are putting dirty clothes in the hamper, putting his plate in the sink after eating, or handing his book bag instead of throwing it on the floor. You get the idea? Choose something that is small and that your child is willing to learn to do.

Ready, Set, Go!

So now that I have gone over most of the basics of toilet training your child, it's time to act. Make sure that you have gathered all of the necessary materials. Make sure that you have discussed this with the significant adults involved in your child's life. Make sure that you have chosen a system to keep a written track of your child's progress.

There are a few more things that we need to talk about before you begin.

1. Your child should no longer wear Pampers or diapers except at night or during times when your child does not have access to the bathroom (for example, when he is on the school bus). Wearing pampers gives your child the message that she is a baby. Wearing underwear gives a more grown-up, responsible message to your child. Your child will more likely feel when she is wet or soiled because underwear does not

absorb like Pampers. If you are concerned about accidents around the house, I suggest that you explore getting plastic pants that your child can wear over his underwear. This way, things are less messy.

2. Once you begin toilet training, all toileting activities should now take place in the bathroom. This includes accidents that your child has when he is wearing a Pamper. This will reinforce to your child that the bathroom is the place for voiding. Changing your child while he lies down passively is promoting dependence.

3. Decide on the names that you will call urination, bowel movements, the bathroom, and the toilet. It is important that you be consistent in the language that you use with your child.

4. There is the question of how often you should prompt your child to the toilet. For those of you who are just starting out, I suggest that for the first week, you prompt

your child to the toilet every half hour. I don't mean every half hour on the half hour. What I mean is going through all the steps of toileting, no matter how long it takes, and then setting the timer for a half hour. This is basically to get you and your child used to the routine. After one week, set the timer for forty-five minutes. You should continue to prompt your child to the bathroom every forty-five minutes until he is accident-free for seven consecutive days. For those of you who have already begun toilet training, you can make a judgement about how often you should prompt your child to the toilet. If your child has not been having so many accidents, you may be able to prompt your child to the bathroom every hour. For those of you who have already started and have not been having much success, then start from the beginning. Don't prompt your child more often than every thirty minutes. Not only is it not practical to prompt your child more often, but it could make toileting unpleasant for your child. It not only fosters dependency, but is not practical to be implemented in a home environment.

5. Besides prompting your child to the bathroom at regular intervals, your child should be prompted to the bathroom as soon as he wakes up, as soon as he comes home from school, and just before he goes to bed at night.

Your follow-up

Decide on a date that you will begin to put your toileting plan into action. Ready, set, go!

Overcoming Obstacles: Getting Unstuck

Toilet training a child with special needs sometimes presents challenges. Some children have sensory issues, especially children diagnosed with Autism Spectrum Disorder. This means being either over or under sensitive to touch, smell, sounds, taste, or sight. Some children have cognitive limitations. This means that they may take a long time to learn a task. Some children have motor issues. Since most of the tasks of toileting require the use of motor skills, this can present an obstacle. Some children have issues with attention, which affects their ability to focus on a task. Some children exhibit challenging behaviors.

It is difficult to teach a child something when he is refusing to follow instructions.

The following are a few of the common problems that I have encountered in the course of my work with families. For each problem, I have given a possible solution. Possible, because each child is unique. In my interventions with families, I always assess the problem before coming up with a solution. However, for those of you experiencing challenges or are stuck, this is meant to give you some ideas about how you may want to proceed.

Problem #1: *My child won't sit on the toilet for even a second.*

Possible Solution: This is definitely a problem since your child has to sit on the toilet long enough to void. Address this problem before you proceed with the rest of the steps of toilet training by desensitizing your child to sitting on the toilet. Start by having your child sit on the toilet for thirty seconds. Help your child to stay seated by putting a hand on his leg or shoulder. Then gradually increase the time until he is able to sit for five minutes. Be sure to praise your child often. Then you can proceed with the rest of toilet training.

Problem #2: *My child refuses to void unless I put on a Pamper. She holds in her bowel movements until I put the Pamper on her. As soon as I put on her Pamper, she has a bowel movement.*

Possible Solution: The good news is that it demonstrates that your child is making a choice. The bad news is that it is not the responsible choice. This can be scary for parents who worry when their child holds their urine or bowel movement for long periods of time. Some parents panic. If this applies to you, then I suggest that you consult with your child's doctor to make sure that your child is not doing any harm to herself. Once that is established, don't give in. Your child is resisting change, which is perfectly normal. Continue to put your child in Pampers only at night or when she does not have access to a bathroom. Do not put a Pamper on your child at any other time. Change takes time. Change can be hard for children, especially children with special needs. Allow your child time to get used to a new way of doing things.

Problem #3: *I am having trouble catching my child's accidents. By the time I take him to the bathroom, he is already wet.*

Possible Solution: As I explained previously, accidents are to be expected. It definitely can be frustrating when your child doesn't seem to be getting the message. There are a few things that you can try.

a. Besides prompting your child to the bathroom at regular planned intervals, prompt your child to the bathroom if he is behaving as if he has to go to the bathroom. Some children get quiet and even hide when they are about to have a bowel movement. You may observe your child wiggling or touching his crotch. The point is that if you observe your child exhibiting any signs that he needs to use the bathroom, you should act immediately.

Make a statement such as: "Johnny, it looks like you have to _______. Let's go to the bathroom." Then prompt your child to the bathroom.

b. If you have noticed any pattern to your child's bowel movements, then you can increase how often you prompt your child to the bathroom during that time period. For example, if your child generally has bowel movements between 6:00 p.m. and 7:30 p.m., then you can prompt him to the bathroom more often during this time frame.

c. Even if you are prompting your child to the bathroom every forty-five minutes, you can check the state of his underwear in between. This is called a dry-pants check. This way, you are increasing the likelihood that you will catch an accident. If your child's pants are dry, then you should praise your child. If your child's pants are wet or soiled, then you should follow the procedure recommended in the last chapter. One or two dry-pants checks in a forty-five-minute period should be sufficient. It is also a good way to help your child distinguish between being wet and being dry.

Problem #4: *My child refuses to go to the bathroom when I ask him to:*

Possible Solution: This is a common problem that parents face. In order to teach your child a new skill, you need his cooperation. When handling a behavior problem, it is important that you remain calm but firm in facial expression and tone of voice. Try the following procedure:

A. Let your child know that he needs to go to the bathroom now.
B. After three requests, you can use a gestural prompt and then try a light physical prompt.
C. Avoid arguing or pleading with your child to go to the bathroom. Avoid physically dragging him to the bathroom. You can use physical guidance if your child begins to cooperate. Also, avoid repeated requests.

This is not only ineffective, but it may lead to a power struggle.

D. If your child still refuses to cooperate, then back off. However, do not allow your child to participate in any other activity until he completes the steps of toileting. This includes playing with toys, tablets, watching television, eating, or drinking. If your child makes any request of you, you can say: "Yes, Johnny, you can ________. But first you have to go to the bathroom and then you can ________."

E. Keep your limit-setting statement brief.

F. Stick to your guns until your child cooperates. Praise your child for his cooperation, no matter how long it takes.

G. Remain consistent. Your child may test you in the beginning. However, he will learn that you are serious if you are consistent. Stick to your guns. Say what you mean and mean what you say!

Problem #5: *My child has learned to use the bathroom and rarely has accidents anymore. But he waits for me to tell him to go to the bathroom and won't tell me when he has to go.*

Possible Solution: The good news is that you and your child have made a considerable amount of progress. Your child has become toilet conditioned. This means that he has learned what the toilet is for and that he needs to void in the toilet and not in his pants. However, being toilet-trained means that he initiates going to the bathroom (by either telling you or going himself). It is common for children with special needs to be prompt-dependent—that is, waiting for instructions. They have been conditioned to wait to be told what to do. Here are some ideas to help your child continue to progress:

a. Make sure that you are not leaving out the communication part of the toileting process. This is a common mistake that parents make, especially as their child has less accidents.

b. Prompt your child to the bathroom less and less often.

c. When you prompt your child to the bathroom, give him a choice. Instead of telling him that it's time to go to the bathroom, ask him if he has to go to the bathroom.

d. Start giving your child choices in other areas of their life. You are teaching him to make decisions and become more independent.

Problem #6: *My child is sixteen years old and still wears Pampers. Is it too late for toilet training?*

Possible Solution: My belief is that it is never too late for a person to learn. I have had success helping parents with adult children with toilet training. Everything that I have suggested so far in the preceding chapters applies, no matter what the age of the child. However, keep in mind that the longer a habit has become ingrained, the more difficult it can be to change. A teenager or adult who has not been toilet trained has become used to being dependent. Therefore, it will require even more patience and commitment.

These are just a few of the obstacles that some parents face when toilet training their child with special needs. These are by no means the only problems. If you are stuck, hopefully, you this gives you some ideas about how you can move forward.

Your follow-up

1. If you are facing any of the obstacles outlined in this chapter, then try some of the suggested possible solutions.
2. Use the Parental Self-Evaluation Checklist (see Appendix C) to identify what you are doing right and what you may need to change.

Some Final Thoughts

What I have shared with you in this book stems from over thirty years of doing in-home and group interventions with parents who have children with special needs. My hope is that you have found this book to be useful to you. My experience is that parents who have been able to put these suggestions into action have been successful. How long it takes and what the journey will look like depends on two things: your child and your commitment. As I said before, each child is an individual, and it is not useful to compare your child with other children.

How much of commitment you are able to make depends on you and the circumstances of your life. If putting all these suggestions into action seems overwhelming, then do part of it. For example, I worked with a single parent whose child with Autism Spectrum Disorder would not sit on the toilet. Her child also presented some challenging behaviors. She was going through a court situation with the child's father and did not feel that she was able to put the full plan into action. However, she was anxious for her child to be toilet trained. We decided that she would begin by doing all toileting activities in the bathroom. She would also prompt him to go inside the bathroom if he behaved as if he had to go to the bathroom. She did not require him to do anything else. She was encouraged by her small success. When she was ready, she put the whole plan into action.

Go at your own pace. Do what you are able to do. If you find that you have to restart, then that's okay. The important thing is to make a commitment to keep things moving. Think of your long-term goals with your child. Imagine what things will be like when your child is toilet trained. This will make it easier to go through the day-to-day challenges.

APPENDIX A

SAMPLE TOILETING DATA SHEET #1

CHILD'S NAME: _______________________________   DATE: _____________

U = Urinate   BM = Bowel Movement

TARGET BEHAVIOR: #1 **In toilet** TARGET BEHAVIOR #2: **Out of toilet**

Morning	#1	#2	Afternoon	#1	#2	Evening	#1	#2
7:00 AM			12:00 PM			5:00 PM		
7:05 AM			12:05 PM			5:05 PM		
7:10 AM			12:10 PM			5:10 PM		
7:15 AM			12:15 PM			5:15 PM		
7:20 AM			12:20 PM			5:20 PM		
7:25 AM			12:25 PM			5:25 PM		
7:30 AM			12:30 PM			5:30 PM		
7:35 AM			12:35 PM			5:35 PM		
7:40 AM			12:40 PM			5:40 PM		
7:45 AM			12:45 PM			5:45 PM		
7:50 AM			12:50 PM			5:50 PM		
7:55 AM			12:55 PM			5:55 PM		
8:00 AM			1:00 PM			6:00 PM		
8:05 AM			1:05 PM			6:05 PM		
8:10 AM			1:10 PM			6:10 PM		
8:15 AM			1:15 PM			6:15 PM		
8:20 AM			1:20 PM			6:20 PM		
8:25 AM			1:25 PM			6:25 PM		
8:30 AM			1:30 PM			6:30 PM		
8:35 AM			1:35 PM			6:35 PM		
8:40 AM			1:40 PM			6:40 PM		
8:45 AM			1:45 PM			6:45 PM		
8:50 AM			1:50 PM			6:50 PM		
8:55 AM			1:55 PM			6:55 PM		

9:00 AM			2:00 PM			7:00 PM		
9:05 AM			2:05 PM			7:05 PM		
9:10 AM			2:10 PM			7:10 PM		
9:15 AM			2:15 PM			7:15 PM		
9:20 AM			2:20 PM			7:20 PM		
9:25 AM			2:25 PM			7:25 PM		
9:30 AM			2:30 PM			7:30 PM		
9:35 AM			2:35 PM			7:35 PM		
9:40 AM			2:40 PM			7:40 PM		
9:45 AM			2:45 PM			7:45 PM		
9:50 AM			2:50 PM			7:50 PM		
9:55 AM			2:55 PM			7:55 PM		
10:00 AM			3:00 PM			8:00 PM		
10:05 AM			3:05 PM			8:05 PM		
10:10 AM			3:10 PM			8:10 PM		
10:15 AM			3:15 PM			8:15 PM		
10:20 AM			3:20 PM			8:20 PM		
10:25 AM			3:25 PM			8:25 PM		
10:30 AM			3:30 PM			8:30 PM		
10:35 AM			3:35 PM			8:35 PM		
10:40 AM			3:40 PM			8:40 PM		
10:45 AM			3:45 PM			8:45 PM		
10:50 AM			3:50 PM			8:50 PM		
10:55 AM			3:55 PM			8:55 PM		
11:00 AM			4:00 PM			9:00 PM		
11:05 AM			4:05 PM			9:05 PM		
11:10 AM			4:10 PM			9:10 PM		
11:15 AM			4:15 PM			9:15 PM		
11:20 AM			4:20 PM			9:20 PM		
11:25 AM			4:25 PM			9:25 PM		
11:30 AM			4:30 PM			9:30 PM		
11:35 AM			4:35 PM			9:35 PM		
11:40 AM			4:40 PM			9:40 PM		
11:45 AM			4:45 PM			9:45 PM		
11:50 AM			4:50 PM			9:50 PM		
11:55 AM			4:55 PM			9:55 PM		

APPENDIX B

SAMPLE TOILETING DATA SHEET #2

Date: _______________   Day of Week: _______________

Time	Prompted by adult?	Went to toilet on his own	U in pants?	BM in pants?	U in toilet?	BM in toilet?	Refused to go?

APPENDIX C

PARENTAL SELF-EVALUATION CHECKLIST

	YES	NO	COMMENTS
Followed steps as outlined in program			
Required child to communicate that they have to go to the bathroom			
Child participated in all the steps of the program			
Allowed child to be as independent in toileting as possible.			
Praised child upon completion of each step of program.			
Praised child extra enthusiastically for voiding in toilet.			
Used egg timer to prompt child to toilet according to time interval agreed upon in program.			
Remained calm during accident procedure.			
Prompted child to follow all steps to toileting after discovering accident.			
Child participated in the accident clean up.			

About the Author

Juliet Hawkins has a master's degree in psychology and is a licensed mental health counselor. She has over thirty-five years of experience working with parents of children with special needs. She has presented at conferences across the country and has conducted workshops for parents and for professionals. Among her specialties are toilet training plans, behavior plans, social stories, and stress management for parents and for individuals with special needs.